Discovering Cultural Japan

Boye De Mente

12306

PASSPORT BOOKS
a division of *NTC Publishing Group*
Lincolnwood, Illinois USA

Cover photo: Dave Bartruff

1992 Printing

Published by Passport Books, a division of NTC Publishing Group,
4255 West Touhy Avenue, Lincolnwood (Chicago), Illinois 60646-1975 U.S.A.
© 1988 by Boye De Mente. All rights reserved. No part of
this book may be reproduced, stored in a retrieval system,
or transmitted in any form, or by any means, electronic,
mechanical, photocopying or otherwise, without the prior
written permission of NTC Publishing Group.
Manufactured in the United States of America.
Library of Congress Catalog Card Number: 87-61242

1 2 3 4 5 6 7 8 9 ML 9 8 7 6 5 4 3

Contents

CHAPTER III

Nihonjin No Kao

Faces of the Japanese

CHAPTER IV

Nihon No Tanoshimi No Koto

The Joys of Japan

CHAPTER V

Bunka No Toge
Crossing the Cultural Barriers

CHAPTER VI

Kogu No Dento
The Traditions of Hospitality

CHAPTER VII

Nihongo
A Little Language Goes a Long Way

CHAPTER VIII

Gochiso-Sama
Pleasuring the Palate

Chapter XIII

Mingeihin

Souvenirs with Soul

Eqilogue

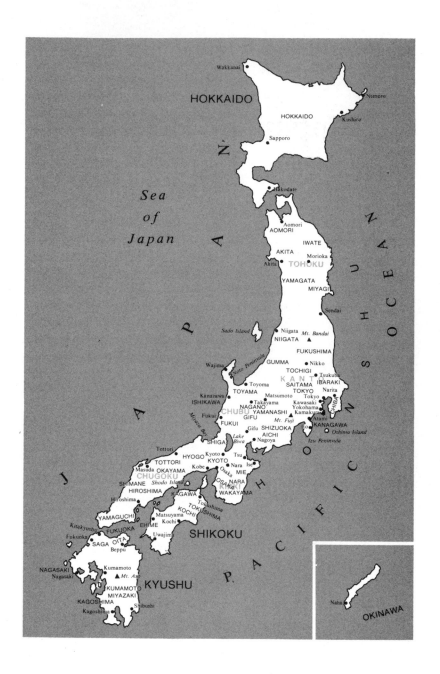

Japan in Profile

Location

Japan is located off the eastern coast of the Asian continent, beginning just below the Russian-held island of
Sakhalin (which adjoins Siberia) and stretching in a south
and southwesterly direction, arc-fashion, from 45 degrees
north latitude to 20 degrees north latitude. From tip to tip,
the island chain is 3,800 kilometers long. At its western-
most point, Japan is only a little more than 100 miles from
Korea on the Asian mainland.

If superimposed over a map of the eastern coast of the
U.S., Japan would stretch from Bangor, Maine, to Jackson-
ville, Florida—and have about the same kind of climate.

Tokyo is 35 degrees north of the equator, and therefore
on approximately the same latitude as Tehran, Athens,
Norfolk, and San Francisco.

Landmass

Japan is made up of four relatively large islands, several
dozen medium-sized ones and thousands of tiny islets, with
a total landmass of 377,765 square kilometers (approxi-

mately 142,000 square miles), which makes it about fifty percent larger than the United Kingdom, a little larger than Norway and Italy, but only one-twenty-fifth the size of the U.S.

Seventy-one percent of Japan is made up of mountains that are mostly uninhabitable. The remaining twenty-nine percent consists of basins and plains.

Population

Japan's population is rapidly approaching the 125-million mark, or around half that of the United States. Approximately twenty-nine million of this number live in Metropolitan Tokyo and the surrounding suburban subcenters, and it is predicted that by the year 2000 this figure will balloon to 34.5 million. Over twenty-two million Japanese live in the Osaka-Kobe-Kyoto area. Since over seventy percent of Japan is mountainous and uninhabited, the total population lives on a land-area that is about the size of some of the larger counties in the American states of Texas, New Mexico, and Arizona.

Japan's population density is 325 persons per square kilometer, compared to 25 in the United States, 110 in China, 353 in the Netherlands, and 672 in Bangladesh.

Government

Japan has a democratic form of government similar to that of England and the United States, with three branches—the legislative, executive, and judicial. The chief executive officer is the prime minister, who is assisted by twenty cabinet ministers. The Diet (similar to Congress and Parliament) is made up of the House of Representatives (511 members) and the House of Councilors (252 members). The Cabinet can dissolve the Diet, and the House of Representatives can pass a motion of nonconfidence in the Cabinet, requiring the appointment of new ministers.

Japan's forty-seven prefectures are administered by governors and assemblies directly elected by residents of the prefectures. There are village, town, and city governments under the prefectural governments.

The judicial system consists of the supreme court, high courts, district courts, family courts, and summary courts.

The emperor of Japan is the symbol of the state but has no powers related to the government. His duties are very much like those of the king or queen of England.

Historical Note

The founding of Japan as a nation is generally given as B.C. 660, when uncorroborated history says the first emperor, Jimmu, was enthroned in what is now Nara Prefecture near Kyoto. Historical records in Korea and China indicate that the Yamato family established itself as the supreme political and military power in Japan, centered in the Nara area, sometime between 200 and 300 A.D. (Yamato was an early name for Japan.) During these centuries, the emperor was both the religious and secular leader of the country.

The primary social organization at that time was the family-related clan, with leadership hereditary. Each of the clan leaders maintained hegemony in their own territories, usually with the advice and consent of the imperial court. The bulk of the people were fishermen, farmers, and hunters.

Contact with nearby Korea and China became common between the third and seventh centuries A.D., resulting in an influx of culture from these two highly advanced civilizations. Architecture, Buddhism, Confucianism, the ideographic system of writing, city planning, ceramic making, lacquering, landscaping, tea, court manners, and apparel styles were just some of the hundreds of concepts, products, and skills that flowed into Japan from the Asian mainland during these long generations.

After some four centuries of absorbing massive amounts of Korean and Chinese culture, the Japanese virtually broke off contact with the mainland and spent the next several hundred years synthesizing and Japanizing the imported technologies and philosophies. The arts, crafts, and literature flourished. Thousands of temples and shrines were built. A road system was extended throughout the country. A new, large capital city was built and named Kyoto.

The imperial family grew into many branches. The imperial court became large and ritualized, with ceremonial pomp and pageantry that rivaled that of the Chinese emperors and Korean kings. Members of the royal families dressed in rich, colorful attire, and spent most of their time in religious, cultural, and recreational pursuits.

As the number of imperial princes and their families grew, the emperor began dispatching some of them to outlying areas as administrators of provincial domains. As the generations passed, these positions became hereditary. The domains became the fiefs of the ruling families, which gradually developed into large clans.

These provincial clan lords imitated the imperial court, with their own religious and political rituals, as well as cultural activities. Life for the privileged classes became highly refined and sophisticated. The sons and daughters of the clan lords enjoyed the titles and the prerogatives of princes and princesses.

Thus it came about that a small minority made up of the imperial family and its branches and the provincial clan lords and ladies lived a life of privileged luxury, supported by the labor of peasant farmers and plebeian craftsmen who had few legal rights and for the most part survived at a subsistence level.

The ties binding the clans to the imperial government continued to loosen. The larger and richer clan lords virtually became independent rulers, with their own armies, and began vying for supreme power. In the late 1100s warfare broke out between the largest of the clans. In 1192 the famous Minamoto clan, under the leadership of Yoritomo Minamoto, defeated the Heike clan and became the primary power in the country. Yoritomo forced the then weak imperial court to appoint him *shogun* (generalissimo), which in effect made him the military dictator of Japan.

This form of government was to endure in Japan until the latter part of the nineteenth century, with a number of relatively long shogunate dynasties succeeding each other after prolonged wars in which competing clans would challenge the power of the shogun, eventually win out, and set up their own shogunate.

The professional warriors maintained by the shogunate and the two hundred-plus provincial fiefs that developed under the new system of government came to be known as *samurai* (sah-muu-rie), from the word, *saburai* (sah-buu-rie), meaning "to guard." The profession of samurai became hereditary, and the samurai families gradually emerged as a new elite, privileged class that was to administer the laws and rules of the clan governments as well as the shogunate until modern times.

By the early 1500s, the ruling Ashikaga shogunate had become so smitten by the cultural refinements of Kyoto that it began to lose military control of the country. Ambitious clan lords in the larger and richer fiefs began contesting for power. In the mid-1500s, Nobunaga Oda emerged as the undisputed military ruler, but before he could consolidate his power and form a new shogunate, he was assassinated. His most capable general, Hideyoshi Toyotomi, who began life as an incorrigible runaway peasant boy and the mascot of a robber gang, quickly defeated Oda's enemies. Because of his lowly origins, there was too much opposition to Hideyoshi having himself named shogun, so he settled for the title of prime minister.

Hideyoshi ruled Japan with an iron hand, and became a patron of the arts and a builder on a massive scale. Among his projects was the great Osaka Castle, which still may be seen today. With his power in Japan absolute and his rebuilding of the nation complete, Hideyoshi sent a huge army to invade and conquer Korea, and then proceed on to China, but he became ill and the army was recalled short of victory. Hideyoshi died before the army could return to Japan.

Ieyasu Tokugawa, Hideyoshi's most ambitious and talented ally, quickly moved to consolidate power in his own hands. After a series of battles against other lords, Ieyasu emerged the winner, and in 1603 established the Tokugawa Shogunate, which was to be Japan's last shogunate dynasty.

Ieyasu moved his headquarters to the small fishing village of Edo at the head of Edo Bay, greatly enlarged a castle that had been built there in the 1400s as a frontier outpost, and set about restructuring the political divisions of the country. Clan lords who had supported him were reconfirmed in their positions and their relations with the new shogunate government. Those who had opposed him were subject to a variety of restrictions designed to keep them in line.

One final battle in 1613 eliminated the family and loyal allies of Hideyoshi Toyotomi, who resented Ieyasu's seizure of power and had continuously intrigued against him since Hideyoshi's death.

The first Westerners had arrived in Japan in 1543, when

a storm blew a Chinese junk off course and it landed on the tiny island of Tanega, twenty miles off the coast of Kyushu, south of the city of Kagoshima. Among the passengers on the ship were three Dutch traders, who had with them guns, tobacco, and syphilis—all three of which were left on the island when they resumed their voyage to Macau.

News of the discovery of a highly civilized island nation off the coast of Korea and China spread rapidly among Europeans in Southeast Asia, and just six years later the first Western missionary, a Jesuit priest named Xavier, arrived in Japan and traded the local clan lords guns and other Western products for permission to preach the Christian religion. Xavier was followed by other missionaries and by traders. Within a few decades there were several hundred foreigners resident in Japan, and many thousands of Japanese had been converted to Christianity.

Word of the warlike nature of the Europeans and their penchant for colonizing less developed countries began to worry Nobunaga Oda. The missionaries in Japan had begun to intrigue against each other, and to favor one clan lord over another with their gifts of guns and other Western things. Nobunaga ordered all missionaries to leave and outlawed the teaching and practice of Christianity. Some missionaries who refused to leave were put to death but the edict was not always enforced.

During the reign of Hideyoshi Toyotomi from 1583 to 1598, actions against missionaries and Japanese Christians were renewed, and many were killed, but once again internal political events distracted Hideyoshi's attention away from the foreigners. Will Adams, the Englishman who was the role model for the pilot in Robert Clavel's famous novel and TV extravaganza *Shogun,* was blown ashore in Japan in 1600, and subsequently became a friend and advisor to Ieyasu Tokugawa, who was to establish the Tokugawa shogunate in 1603.

Problems with missionaries and foreigners continued

following Ieyasu's retirement and death in 1616. Finally, Ieyasu's grandson, Iemitsu, closed Japan off from the rest of the world in 1637, ordering all foreigners out of the country and decreeing the death sentence for anyone, including Japanese who happened to be abroad at that time, who attempted to enter Japan.

The only exception to this law was a small Dutch-operated trading post on a man-made island called *Dejima* (day-je-mah) in Nagasaki harbor. The Dutch were allowed to keep a few traders there and to bring in one ship a year for the exchange of goods. Chinese traders were also allowed limited access to Japan through the post.

This single tiny window to the outside world was the only official contact Japan was to have with the West until the 1850s, when America's Commodore Perry arrived with his squadron of black warships and delivered an ultimatum to the aging Tokugawa shogunate to open Japan to foreign trade, or else.

In the intervening years of the Tokugawa Period, Edo had grown into one of the largest cities on earth. Japanese culture had flourished and evolved into one of the world's most distinctive civilizations. But the country was still a feudalistic society of lords, ladies, sword-carrying warriors, peasants, and plebeians, such as had not been seen in Europe and the U.S. for many generations.

Opening Japan to the outside world resulted in the fall of the Tokugawa shogunate, the formation of a parliamentary type of government, and the rapid industrialization and modernization of the country. Victorious in a war against China in 1895 and against Russia in 1904–1905, the Japanese quickly emerged on the international scene as a formidable people—highly disciplined and educated, and determined to catch up with and surpass the West at its own game of industrial and military hegemony.

These ultranationalistic motives led the Japanese to the

debacle of World War II, which, as destructive and as tragic as it was, opened the way for genuine democracy and individual freedom in Japan, and loosed a torrent of Japanese talent and ambition that has propelled them into the front ranks of the world's peoples.

The Addressing System in Japan

Most streets in Japan are not named, and the addressing system has nothing to do with streets. Instead it is based on areas that differ in shape and size. Homes and buildings within these areas are numbered, but because of the irregular shapes of the areas, the numbers may not be in sequence on the same street-front for more than a hundred yards or so, and then the sequence continues somewhere behind that line of buildings. There may be fifty or more buildings jammed together in one area that is the equivalent of three or four square blocks, so there would be several "lines," often not straight, of sequential numbers.

Larger cities in Japan are divided into wards (ku), which are further divided into smaller areas with a variety of names such as Nihonbashi, Aoyama, Sakamachi, etc., which in turn may or may not be divided into areas called chome (choe-may) that are subdivided into yet smaller sections called banchi (bahn-chee). A typical address in Tokyo is: Tokyo, Shibuya Ward, 6 chome, 1-28 banchi. This means the twenty-eighth building in banchi number one, which is part of the sixth chome in Shibuya. Another version of a Tokyo address is: Chiyoda Ward, Kojimachi, 4 chome, 3-10 banchi—the tenth building in banchi number three, in the fourth chome in the area known as Kojimachi, which is one of dozens of named areas in Chiyoda Ward.

If this sounds complicated, it is. The secret of finding addresses in Tokyo and in Japan in general is to determine their location in relation to some well-known transportation terminal or station, intersection, park, shrine, major building, or some other landmark. Once you are in the vicinity of the landmark you begin to look for the name and number of the area on small plaques posted on telephone or other poles along the street or on the fronts of buildings. There is no particular uniformity of size or style for address signs so it is often necessary to search for them. Many homes and buildings, especially larger office buildings and government buildings, do not have address signs posted anywhere. If you don't know the name of the building you are looking for you have to ask someone—often someone who works in the building—if that is the proper building or address.

Best thing to do before you start out for a new address is have someone draw a detailed location map for you (by calling the address concerned and getting specific guidelines, if necessary). Or, if you are going by taxi, to have the address and location written out in Japanese to hand to the driver. Hotel and inn staffs in Japan are old hands at this important service.

Introduction

Putting the Fun Back into Travel

For several decades the international travel industry has concentrated much of its effort and money on taking the unfamiliar—and consequently much of the adventure and pleasure—out of traveling abroad.

If this sounds like a contradiction, you're right. It is. Everyone knows that going abroad as a tourist is supposed to be adventurous and fun as well as educational.

Of course, the travel industry is not deliberately being contrary or uncaring. The principle it has been following is to provide travelers with the kind and quality of accommodations and food they are used to at home—if not better. Along with this just-like-home service come guides, interpreters, and others who look after the needs and desires of travelers to the extent that about all the travelers have to do is feed and bathe themselves and do their own shopping (although *all* of *these* services are also available to the traveler who wants to take advantage of them).

The unfortunate thing, of course, is that this sanitized and homogenized system isolates the traveler from the personal experiences that make traveling worthwhile and memorable. Wrapped in the womb of the system from beginning to end, the traveler becomes little more than an arm's-length observer.

Because of this system, many travelers make no effort to learn anything about the country they are going to visit. Their trip abroad thus becomes little more than a physical interlude spent mostly on planes and buses and in hotels, with a series of images they glimpse in passing. One might be better off watching a good travel video at home. It's much cheaper and there is no jet lag.

But if you have the means, the time, and the imagination to travel abroad, you owe it to yourself to get as much as possible out of the trip.

It is my contention that Japan is one of the greatest travel experiences in the world today for anyone who is willing to learn a little about the country and expose himself or herself to its pleasures.

The Japanese are exceedingly courteous, friendly, and hospitable (with none of the arrogance or snobbery that is frequently encountered in some countries I could name). They routinely go beyond expectations in their efforts to help visitors enjoy their country.

Japan is rich in natural scenery. Great expanses of the country are so gorgeous they captivate the senses and the spirit.

Japanese cuisine offers an extensive variety of dishes of gourmet quality that may be hard to pronounce and have a different look, but are nevertheless delicious and nutritious, and are worth adding to your daily diet.

The traditional lifestyle of the Japanese offers the visitor an opportunity for new experiences that are the achievements of a highly sophisticated, distinctive culture that has been continuous for over two thousand years.

The aesthetic and metaphysical arts of Japan are based on classic, universal principles that please the mind and nurture the spirit—and are readily available to the visitor who has even a little advance knowledge and the smallest amount of energy and interest.

This book is designed to provide you with the historical and cultural perspective, the insights and the knowledge you need to intellectually, emotionally, and physically cross the cultural barriers into the inner circle of Japanese life and savor it to the fullest extent possible.

There are, in fact, two Japans. One is the product of modern industry and is therefore similar to other highly industrialized countries. The other is the Japan of the past—the "Traditional Japan" that traces its beginnings back more than twenty-five hundred years. It is this traditional world that makes Japan a unique experience for the visitor from abroad. The visitor is able to move freely back and forth between the two ways of life, enjoying the best of both just as the Japanese do.

My own love affair with Japan began when I was twenty years old, and my ardor has increased with the years. There have been ups and downs, of course, as in any passionate relationship, but as a mistress Japan is incomparable. No matter how many loves may come afterward, none ever entirely replaces her.

I am not alone.

Almost everyone who has spent more than a few days in Japan has succumbed to some degree to its fascination. And, like myself, most who spend any considerable time there find their lives permanently changed.

What is this spell that Japan casts upon even the most jaded traveler? What is it, exactly, that makes Japan so different, so much of an "out of this world" experience? The answer to this question is found in the distinctive attitudes and etiquette of the Japanese and in the style of living they developed during their long history.

In its idealized form, this style of living, known as *The Japanese Way,* came close to fulfilling the sensual, intellectual, and spiritual needs of man. The primary goal of the system was harmony—among men and between men and nature. The lifestyle included the practicing of a highly refined system of manners, humility, hospitality, generosity, and instinctive unselfishness.

The Japanese Way also included an extraordinarily well-developed sense of aesthetic taste in matters relating to architecture, interior decoration, handicrafts, and even in the serving of food. There were numerous contemplative exercises designed to contribute to mental and spiritual maturity. There was also a relaxed, natural attitude toward sensual pleasures.

This unique mode of living is still maintained by vast numbers of Japanese, although the majority now follow the old traditional way only on a part-time basis. In the cities it is to be found in numerous private homes, in purely Japanese-style restaurants, in inns, and in thousands of temples and shrines. It is still the rule rather than the exception in a majority of rural homes; and the farther one gets from the great urban areas, the more traditional becomes the style of living.

For the growing number of urban Japanese who now live more or less Western-style, the traditional-style inns and restaurants provide the primary link with the past. These inns and restaurants also provide the visiting foreigner with the same opportunity to experience *The Japanese Way.*

Few Westerners can spend even a day in the traditional setting of Japan without being powerfully affected by the spell of its unique charm. After a while, the lure of the traditional Japanese lifestyle begins to exercise an attraction on many that is almost mystic.

I have tried in this book to help the reader both see and feel Japan in four dimensions—its physical beauty, its humanity, its spirit, and its special pleasures. To get to really know any country not your own requires the use of more than the five common senses. One must have a special intuitive sense to absorb the finer nuances of another culture.

I have always felt that I had this extrasensory perception in regard to Japan (in fact, deep in my mind I have the nagging notion that I once *was* Japanese). So my aim here has also been to share with you at least some of the enjoyment this special affinity gives me—and hopefully, to influence you to go to Japan to see and feel for yourself.

CHAPTER I

Kami-Sama No Kuni
Land of the Gods

The Age of the Gods

According to early chronicles and myths, the Japanese islands were created by a god and a goddess, *Izanagi* (ee-zah-nah-ghee) and *Izanami* (ee-zah-nah-me), who so admired their own handiwork that they descended from heaven to live on the islands. The godly couple then gave birth to the gods of the sun and the moon, of storms and of fire, and finally to lesser *kami* (kah-me) gods who became the ancestors of the Japanese.

This ancient legend establishes very early in their history that the Japanese were overwhelmingly impressed with the stunning natural beauty of their land, and that they also regarded themselves as extraordinary people. They were right in both instances.

The early Japanese believed that all natural objects and phenomena were ordained with some degree of divine spirit, and that it was necessary to live in harmony with nature in order to avoid upsetting the natural balance. Their reverence for nature and beauty was to permeate the Japanese way of life from top to bottom, and to color the

1

entire cultural fabric down to the present time.

Historically speaking, Japan's "Age of the Gods" ended in B.C. 660 when the "grandson" of the Sun Goddess became the master of southern and central Japan by force of arms, and set himself up as *Tenno* (tane-no), which is usually translated as "Emperor," but means the "Royal Son of Heaven."

The common people in the new kingdom (those who could not trace their ancestry directly to *kami*) were known as *ryomin* (rio-mean) or "good people." And at that time, the main body of Japanese called their country *Yamato* (yah-mah-toe) or "Great Peace." This later became *Nihon* (nee-hone) or *Nippon* (neep-pone), which means "Source of the Sun" (as seen from China). It is the Chinese form of *Nippon*, namely *Jih-pen*, that the modern word "Japan" comes from.

The Land the Gods Created

The most outstanding physical feature of "the lands the gods created" is its great mountain chains, its towering volcanic peaks, and the relatively broad plains on the islands of Honshu (hone-shuu) and Hokkaido (hoke-kie-doe). Much to the surprise of most visitors, four-fifths of Japan (which is larger than Italy and only slightly smaller than France) is made up of mountains of natural and volcanic origin, with an immense range running through each of the major islands.

To get a good idea of the topography of the islands, imagine each one of them with a high backbone of mountains in the center and ranges of smaller mountains radiating outward toward the coasts. Rivers originating in the mountains flow down the opposite sides, forming numerous narrow valleys and small coastal plains that are separated from each other by rugged ridges and headlands.

On the main island of Honshu, the greatest of these natural mountain ranges, characterized by sheer cliffs and peaks up to nine thousand feet in height, are known as the Northern, Central, and Southern Alps—because of their similarity to the Alps of Switzerland. While these and other natural mountains of Japan are among the world's grandest beauty spots, it is the volcanic mountains that provide the special flavor of the country's topography.

Altogether, there are seven large volcanic systems (with nearly two hundred volcanoes) running through the islands. The best known of these, of course, is the Mt. Fuji system, which begins in Niigata (nee-gah-tah) Prefecture northwest of Tokyo, includes the *Hakone* (hah-koe-nay) Mountains, the mountains of the *Izu* (ee-zoo) Peninsula south of Tokyo, the Seven Isles of Izu, Mt. Mihara on Oshima Island in Tokyo Bay, and goes all the way to Guam in the Pacific Ocean.

The great plains of Japan are the *Kanto* (kahn-toe) which surrounds Tokyo and Yokohama; the *Niigata* (nee-gah-tah) in Niigata Prefecture; the *Nobi* (no-bee) around Nagoya and Gifu City; the *Sendai* (sen-die) in northeastern Honshu; and the *Ishikari* (ee-she-kah-ree) in Hokkaido. The important cities of Kyoto, Yamagata, and Kofu are in great basins.

One of Japan's most impressive and inspiring sights is any one of a dozen of the famous views of Mt. Fuji, its tallest mountain, which at 12,365 feet stands over the islands like a national monument symbolizing the spirit and purpose that unite the country.

The Fabulous Coasts, Rivers, and Lakes

The divine creators of Japan also outdid themselves when they fashioned the coastlines. Altogether Japan has 16,120 miles of seacoast that alternates between white-sand beaches bordered by groves of gnarled green pines, precipitous cliffs also clad in pines, lagoon-like bays dotted with emerald islets, secluded coves and inlets bounded by jagged walls of stone, along with caves, caverns, natural "bridges" and "gates" sculpted from fantastic rock formations. There are unsurpassed seascapes which include numerous offshore islands anchored in blue water and ringed with surf breaking white on black rocks.

Without exaggeration, seemingly unending stretches of Japan's coastline are so extraordinarily beautiful that many who are more finely attuned find themselves intoxicated by the sight.

Another source of aesthetic intoxication in Japan are the bountiful rivers and streams (excluding the larger ones where they pass through great industrial cities—the *Yodo* (yoe-doe) in Osaka and the *Sumida* (sue-me-dah) in Tokyo). Being exceedingly mountainous with high rain and snow falls, Japan has hundreds of rivers and streams, but they are mostly short and swift. The longest river is the *Shinano* (she-nah-no), which begins at the foot of *Mt. Kobushi* (koe-buu-she) north of Tokyo, and enters the Sea of Japan at Niigata City, 229 miles away. The *Tone* (toe-nay), which begins in the *Tango* (tahn-go) Mountains and flows into the sea at Choshi adjoining Tokyo, is responsible for the largest river basin in Japan and is only two hundred miles long.

Because of the tree-covered mountain terrain, particularly in the areas that are volcanic in origin, the majority of Japan's streams and rivers pass through regions of unbounded beauty. Many are marked by rapids that provide some of the most exciting riverboating in the world. Some of the rivers that have mountain lakes as their sources drop in cascades, like canal locks in reverse, down to the sea. Literally hundreds of these streams, their waters sparkling clear and cool even in midsummer, rush through deep, heavily wooded gorges that have a rare beauty which seems unique to Japan.

Practically all of Japan's famous resort spas are located on, or within a short distance from, a river or stream, on a site especially picked for its exceptional beauty. A number that I have been to are built over trout-filled streams, allowing guests to fish from their lanais; streams, filled with huge multicolored carp, take circuitous courses through enclosed garden patios.

Japan is also rich in lakes, many formed by water collecting in volcanic calderas and by the damming of rivers by ancient lava flows. The largest of the lakes is *Biwa* (bee-wah)—260 square miles—near Kyoto. The deepest lake (1,275 feet) is *Tazawa* (tah-zah-wah) in northern Honshu.

Among the most famous of Japan's lakes are the five looped around the waist of Mt. Fuji. The queen of these is *Ashi* (ah-she), popularly known as Lake Hakone because it is high in the Hakone Mountains. Lying deep in a giant tree-lined crater, with Mt. Fuji looming majestically over it like a stairway to the heavens, Lake Hakone is frequently ringed with snow in the winter and often mist-shrouded in all seasons. Just as often it leaves its viewers speechless with admiration of its beauty.

The Kaleidoscope of Color

A great part of the natural beauty of Japan is provided by its colors, which are tuned to the seasons. The primary color of Japan is some nuance of green—leaf green, pine-needle green, grass green, or grain green, the latter waxing and waning from spring to fall. The other color that is permanently on display is the brilliant blue of the coastal waters, attached to the beaches, headlands, and sea-cliffs by ribbons of frothy white.

The next most conspicuous color is that of the snow that blankets great expanses of Hokkaido and Honshu for months during the winter, turning the tree-covered mountains and open tablelands into shimmering seas of crystal white. Then there are the hues of fall, which stir the Japanese soul with their message of the fate of all living things.

First to herald the approach of fall are the quilt-patch paddy fields of rice which ripen to a dusky yellow. Then beginning in Hokkaido and moving south, as sap withdraws from trees to begin the winter-long hibernation, large segments of Japan's mantle of green leaves change color like so many chameleons, and almost before your eyes forests of fir, spruce, beech, maple, and other species blush brilliant shades of red, gold, and brown. For several weeks thereafter, Japan is a kaleidoscope of colors, as the plumage of autumn competes for a while with the remaining coat of evergreens.

Another source of color that adds so much to the distinctive Japanese countryside are roofing tiles. Especially as you travel by train from Tokyo toward Kyoto and other southwestern destinations, you pass above clusters of homes, in fields and in innumerable glens and glades, that are topped with eye-catching patterns of ceramic tile cast in deep blue, purple, aquamarine, or pastel tints that delight the eye.

Altogether, the distinctive topography and the exceptional natural beauty of the islands of Japan provide a key ingredient in the unique culture that has developed on them.

CHAPTER II

Kisetsu No Bunka
The Seasonal Culture

The Siberian Winds

Another important key to understanding and appreciating Japan is knowing the role that climate has played in shaping the attitudes and character of the people, and how it traditionally related to their everyday life.

From the northern tip of Hokkaido (from which the Russian-held Siberian island of Sakhalin is visible) to Kagoshima on the southern edge of Kyushu, Japan stretches some 1,860 miles in a north to southwesterly direction. Hokkaido is at approximately the same latitude as the state of Maine in the U.S., and has similar weather—cool summers and long, cold winters with an abundance of snow.

The main island of Honshu parallels the eastern seaboard of the U.S. from about New York down to South Carolina, but the island has two distinct types of weather. The great ridge of mountains that run more or less north-south down the center of the island serves as a barrier blocking the cold, moisture-laden winter winds that sweep across the narrow Sea of Japan from Siberia, causing them to lose their water content in the form of snow on the west

7

side of this barrier and atop the mountains themselves. This area is Japan's fabled *Yuki Guni* (yuu-kee guu-nee) or "Snow Country," where deep snows are the main fact of life from late November to April each year.

The South Pacific Current

In addition to the protection offered by the great mountain barrier, the side of Japan facing the Pacific Ocean has another benefactor—the famous *Kuroshio* (kuu-roe-she-oh), or "Black Current," which streams up from the South Pacific, bathing the eastern seaboard in warming waters. The *Miura* (mee-uu-rah) and *Izu* (ee-zoo) peninsulas, which protrude out into this warm current just south of Tokyo, enjoy a mostly mild winter climate that has made them famous for centuries.

Official pronouncements on the subject of Japan's weather—which are often faithfully repeated in travel literature—state that Japan has a "mild" climate. This is true only in a relative sense, and then only in certain southern districts.

Winters on the Pacific side of the islands from Kagoshima at the southern tip of Kyushu to about one hundred miles north of Tokyo are distinguished by dry, sunny days alternating with short rainy, windy periods. As one moves inland and northward, light snows at lower altitudes and heavier snows in the mountains are characteristic. Temperatures even in the southern regions and along the coast may be mild one day and very cold the next.

Spring throughout the islands is changeable. Sunny clear days alternate with light to heavy rains that may continue for days. There is considerable rainfall from around the end of May to early July. Summer brings hot, humid days at lower altitudes throughout the southern islands and on Honshu as far north as the jumping-off point for Hokkaido. Typhoons, in the form of heavy rains and winds, regularly sweep the islands from late summer to early November, with September being "Typhoon Month."

In the southern and central portions of the islands, autumn brings many clear, cool days, and is generally the most comfortable time of the year. Northern Honshu and Hokkaido have brief, crisp autumns, with snow beginning in the mountains as early as October.

The four seasons in Japan are thus very pronounced, and the Japanese have always been acutely aware of this. Popular writer Shunkichi Akimoto, in his delightful book, *Exploring the Japanese Ways of Life,* says theirs is a "seasonal culture" and that their "season mindedness" is one of the primary characteristics of the Japanese. To even vaguely appreciate the traditional manifestations of Japanese thought and behavior, one must be familiar with this seasonal culture.

The Golden Tranquility of Fall

Apparently long before the Japanese began recording their history, they had already developed as a national characteristic a delicate sense of the seasons that colored every phase and facet of their lives. Until the end of the last century there was hardly any thought or action that was not somehow hinged to one of the seasons. As Akimoto-san says, there was literally a proper season for almost everything.

Because of their vivid awareness of the fragility and impermanence of life, and probably because it also meant relief from the heat and humidity of summer, the Japanese have always been especially attracted to autumn. The early morning and evening chill of the air, the leaves beginning to change color, the shortening of the shadows at sunset, and perhaps (in the words of Shunkichi Akimoto) "a flight of wild geese cruising across the skies forming a long two-line wedge headed by a queen or kingly leader" were tinged with an exquisite sadness that struck an exceptionally responsive chord in the soul of the Japanese.

Probably the best-known autumn custom, which began in Japan in prehistoric times and has continued down to the present-day, is that of celebrating the beauty of the full fall moon—popularly known as "Moon-Viewing." The moon-viewing ceremony traditionally included making special offerings to household shrines, eating special foods, and exchanging delicacies with friends and neighbors—practices that have waned considerably in recent decades, but are still followed by a devoted few.

The highlight of moon-viewing is a gathering of a few select friends at some spot where the view of the moon is extraordinarily impressive, to eat and drink, and while gazing at the moon, to compose poetry honoring its special beauty.

One can get a good idea of the popularity and importance of this custom from the fact that hundreds of places around the country have been noted as moon-viewing spots for centuries.

There are two particularly expressive Japanese words that are intimately associated with fall: *sabishii* (sah-bee-shee) and *shinmiri* (sheen-me-ree). The first of these words means "loneliness" plus a type of "emptiness" which is used to describe the feeling that often assails the more sensitive Japanese with the coming of the first signs of fall. The Japanese do not try to avoid or relieve this feeling of loneliness or emptiness. They cater to it. Moon-viewing, insect-hearing (listening to the singing of insects), and autumnal pilgrimages to remote mountain shrines—popular fall pastimes—are fraught with the sense of studied melancholy which serves to repair the life-worn spirits of the Japanese.

Shinmiri is also a commonly used colloquial word and refers to a type of atmosphere that is charged with intimate tranquility and sad contentment which is characteristic of Japan's traditional lifestyle. As expressed in my book, *Japanese Secrets of Graceful Living:* "The idea of passing time alone, austerely, while letting one's mind dwell on nostalgic events of the past, or giving up the hectic life of the city for a quiet rustic type of existence in some isolated countryside is not unique to Japan, but no other people crave it like the Japanese. As a result of this craving, the Japanese attempt to create the atmosphere in their surroundings, their music, and their literature.

"Rain is often one of the most important ingredients of a *shinmiri* atmosphere. An afternoon spent sitting quietly in a Japanese-style room that looks out over a garden, field, or valley that is being pelted by a late fall rain is certain to be flooded with a strong feeling of *shinmiri*."

The Mystique of Winter

Until about 1950 the Japanese seemed to have regarded their climate as semitropical if not tropical, and often appeared to ignore the low temperatures of winter. Homes were not built to retain heat and no effort was made to heat them. All during winter in Tokyo and other cities of central and southern Japan (except during blowing rainstorms) the custom was (and still is in many homes) to open all windows and outside sliding doors the first thing in the morning and leave them open for several hours.

On the coldest days, porcelain *hibachi* (he-bah-chee) braziers filled with smoldering charcoal were used to warm the hands. In more affluent homes, *hibachi* were also placed in covered pits in the floor called *kotatsu* (koe-taht-sue) into which one extended his legs and arms for warmth. Everyone wore several layers of clothing to keep the body warm.

Rather than trying to ward off winter with its rigors, the Japanese found ways to enjoy its special aspects. The two most noted winter customs, practiced as national observances, were *yuki-mi* (yuu-kee-me), or snow-viewing, and plum blossom-viewing. Among the upper classes, the first snow of the year was marked by groups getting together at special places to admire its beauty and compose *haiku* (hie-kuu) poetry commemorating the transcendental beauty of the fragile crystals.

One of the most attractive and common types of stone lanterns found in the gardens of private homes and inns was designed to be lighted during or following snowfalls so that occupants could enjoy the sight even at night. Snow thus became a means for the Japanese to practice aesthetic appreciation.

Plum blossom-viewing, in March when the trees are in full bloom, was a popular custom as far back as 800 A.D., and although considerably diminished, remains today an important exercise in aestheticism for many Japanese. The blossoms, appearing naked and fragile amidst the snow and wind of late winter, are said by Shunkichi Akimoto to symbolize for the Japanese the virtues of chastity, courage, and austerity under adverse conditions.

Another winter scene that the Japanese have traditionally admired, and around which they developed specific customs, was the combining of snow with sprigs of pine, bamboo, and plum in numerous decorative functions.

Today, the main winter celebration is *Oshogatsu* (oh-show-got-sue), New Years, which is marked by visits to shrines and the homes of relatives and friends, giving gifts, eating special foods, and visiting ancestral homes. On New Year's night, hundreds of thousands of people flock to noted shrines in their area to mark the end of the old year and the beginning of the new.

At some of the great shrines around the country, hundreds of young men, usually dressed only in loincloths despite the generally frigid temperatures, participate in bell-ringing ceremonies that are televised nationally and provide one of the most exciting spectacles to be seen in Japan. Some of these temple bells are immense in size, with their clappers consisting of giant logs suspended on ropes from the ceiling. There is nothing quite like the far-carrying sound of one of these great bells, and to me there is no more poignant reminder of how intimately Japan's present is linked with its past.

The Cherry Blossom Spring

For nearly a thousand years the coming of spring in Japan has been marked by parties held beneath canopies of cherry trees. In earlier centuries, some of the greatest social and cultural events in the country's history were cherry blossom parties held at famous viewing places. References to cherry blossoms in the novels and poetry of Japan are legend.

The fragile pink petals of the cherry tree long ago came to symbolize for the Japanese not only the incomparable beauty of nature but also the impermanence of all things, especially the tenuous hold man has on life. Formal occasions to celebrate the beauty and characteristics of the blossoms first developed among the privileged classes in the eleventh century, and by the 1600s had spread downward to include the common people.

Eventually cherry blossom-viewing became a genuine cult and was just as influential in its own way as the more famous "Cult of the Sword" which developed around the use of that weapon during the long supremacy of Japan's *Samurai* warrior class from 1192 A.D. until recent times. In no other country has a blossom ever played such an imposing role.

Still today, millions of Japanese each spring hold outings beneath the short-lived blossoms. Women dress in their gayest kimono. Box lunches, along with spiritous drinks, are taken or bought on the spot from mobile vendors. Except among the more serious aesthetes, these parties are not sedate, calm affairs at which the participants sit around quietly contemplating the beauty and fragility of the blossoms and tossing off equally fragile poetry. The majority of the occasions have traditionally been accompanied by unrestrained indulgence in *O'sake* (oh-sah-kay) rice wine, especially by men, who take the lead in singing popular folksongs and dancing.

This popular sensual and aesthetic celebration usually begins in Kagoshima on the southern end of Kyushu in late March and advances up the island chain with the season, ending in Hokkaido in June.

In Tokyo some of the more famous cherry blossom-viewing spots include Shinjuku Gyoen Gardens, Ueno Park, and Chidorigafuchi Park. The huge Imperial Palace grounds in the center of Tokyo are also ringed by cherry trees, providing passersby with the opportunity to enjoy the beauty of the blossoms daily for several days without going out of their way.

One of the most noted cherry blossom-viewing spots in the Kyoto area is Arashi Mountain on the outskirts of the city. Probably the most famous viewing place in the country is at Yoshino in Nara Prefecture, an hour from either Osaka or Kyoto, where an entire valley and mountainside are covered with a profusion of cherry trees. The trees, numbering around 100,000 and appearing in four groves, were first planted in the latter part of the seventh century by a priest named En-no-Ozunu.

The Season to Be *Assari*

The style of life that the Japanese developed for summer is closely associated with the word *assari* (ahs-sah-ree), which means "simple, frank, brief," and "light-hearted and relaxed." Among the summer cooling diversions—*suzumi* (sue-zoo-me)—were swimming, fishing, mountain-hiking, strolling along rivers and mountain streams, eating light meals, thinking light thoughts, attending open-air theatrical performances and neighborhood festivals, relating ghost stories to send chills up each other's backs, and attending ghost plays at theaters.

The summer *assari* customs that were especially popular in the evenings, after the day's work was done, are described by the word *yusuzumi* (yuu-sue-zoo-me), which means something like "enjoying the cool of the evening." To practice *yusuzumi* it was first of all necessary for one to wipe his mind clean of all events of the day just ending. The next step was to take a hot bath followed by a drenching in cool water, then don a clean *yukata* (yu-kah-tah) robe and take up a small fan that had been delicately scented with the aroma of pine.

Once a person had cleansed both body and mind, he was ready for the next step—idle contemplation. While contemplating, he might sit and listen to the sounds peculiar to a summer evening—birds in the trees, insects in the garden grass, children playing in the distance, the tinkling of a windbell, or the gurgle of running water. One could stroll in his garden or along the banks of a nearby stream.

The idea was to relax completely and refresh one's self by forgetting all worldly cares so that the discomfort of the summer heat would disappear into the lengthening shadows.

Certainly not all Japanese follow these traditional summer practices of *yusuzumi* today. In urban areas, most have air-conditioning in their homes or apartments. But there are those who do, especially in rural areas and suburbs of the cities, and the attitude remains strongly entrenched.

One of the most popular and enduring of the *yusuzumi* practices of Japan is watching and participating in the colorful *Bon Odori* (bone oh-doe-ree) or Bon Dance, which is a type of community folk-dancing that originated centuries ago in relation to ancestor worship. Although its religious connotations have been forgotten, it is still performed throughout Japan during mid-July in urban areas and in mid-August in the countryside.

A temporary bandstand, usually elevated on high poles, is erected in the neighborhood temple grounds. The area is festooned with colorful paper lanterns and bunting. Music is provided by a group dressed in traditional costumes—or in some cases today, by a tape deck. Residents of the neighborhood, mostly dressed in the cool, comfortable *yukata*, gather at the grounds at about dusk, and for the next two or three hours watch, stroll about, and dance to the nostalgic, haunting melodies of Old Japan.

In many areas near water, the annual Obon Festival includes *Toro Nagashi* (toe-roe nah-gah-she), or "the Floating of the Lanterns," during which small candlelit lanterns on tiny rafts are set loose on the water.

CHAPTER III

Ninhonjin No Kao
Faces of the Japanese

The People Make the Difference

During the many years that I have been connected with Japan and intimately concerned with the country as a travel area, it has been my experience that an overwhelming majority of the well-traveled people who go there for pleasure later say it is by far the best; that no other country compares. When questioned in detail about why they feel this way, most of the travelers finally end up saying, "Because the people are so wonderful."

My own opinion is that the unique appeal of Japan is a combination of the character and customs of the people, the distinctive food, the traditional dress, the Japanese inn, the aesthetic charm of the arts and crafts, and so on. But I have also personally known dozens of Westerners who did not appreciate any of these latter things and yet stayed on in Japan for years, unwilling to leave despite their many dislikes.

While it would be easy to dismiss this particular group as being attracted to Japan only because of the cultural emphasis on sex and the sexual permissiveness they are able to participate in, this would not be the whole truth and would be unfair to my friends and acquaintances as well as to the Japanese. For there is actually a great deal more than sexual pleasure involved in the relationships these people have with Japan, and one way or another it can all be traced to the traditional character, personality, and manners of the people.

The Japanese are extraordinarily conscious of their racial differences and of their distinctive culture, and they habitually distinguish between what is "native" and what has been imported from the West. These same differences are also very conspicuous to the Western visitor, who often is even more inclined to discriminate between what he perceives to be Japanese and non-Japanese. One result of this situation is that both the faults and the good points of the Japanese and "things Japanese" are constantly being emphasized. Of course, it is the "good points" that exercise an almost hypnotic attraction on the visitor from abroad.

Racial Heritage of the Japanese

It is generally agreed that the Japanese are a mixture of four racial groups: two distinctively Mongoloid groups from the mainland of Asia; a Malay-Negrito stock from Southeast Asia who first settled in Kyushu; and the *Ainu* (aye-new), a Caucasoid race who were apparently the original inhabitants of the islands (possibly from the age when the islands were still attached to the Asian continent).

Contrary to a common stereotyped image, the Japanese do not all look alike, although there are fewer extremes in their general appearance and features than are seen in the U.S. and most European countries.

The Japanese generally have black or deep auburn colored hair, slender builds, and the characteristic Oriental eye to varying degrees. Beyond this there are conspicuous differences in height, complexion, individual facial features, and figures. For the average Westerner it requires only a few hours, or days at most, to switch from identifying individuals by their body builds, hair color, and voice to looking more closely at the finer features of their faces.

For a racial and ethnic group that has been called physically unattractive by some of its own artists and writers who have lived and traveled abroad (the most celebrated case being a former ambassador who wrote a book in which he said his fellow countrymen reminded him of monkeys), Japan has traditionally produced some of the world's more beautiful women—by anyone's standards. The Kyoto and Tohoku areas are especially noted for the extraordinary beauty of their women.

At any rate, the faces and figures of the Japanese have been undergoing remarkable changes since the 1950s, and old descriptions are no longer valid. Younger generations are taller and heavier than their parents. The figures of the girls are becoming more voluptuous and those of the boys more muscular.

The Shinto Theme in Japanese Character

Shintoism, the native religion, played a vital role in shaping the basic character of the Japanese, and subsequently the unique Japanese civilization. The myth of the divine origin of Japan and the Japanese, which stands at the center of Shintoism, has already been mentioned. Other essential facets of Shintoism include a deep reverence for all aspects of nature from both a spiritual and an aesthetic viewpoint, along with a special concern for the fertility of living things. Fertility festivals were common until recent times, and still may be seen in both urban and rural areas around the country. Phallic symbols, especially the erect male organ, were common throughout the islands at intersections of roads and other well-traveled places.

Shintoism stresses ritual purity, and is a cheerful, optimistic, happy religion. Its festivals are more like carnivals than religious observances. Food stalls, booths selling souvenirs and novelty items, singing, dancing, and drinking are characteristic of Shinto festivals.

In Shintoism, mountains are regarded as sacred places because, according to ancient myths, they are where souls go after death. This belief led to the building of shrines on mountain tops and in high places in general, from hills to even low mounds rising abruptly out of level plains.

The ranking Shinto shrine in Japan is the *Grand Shrine of Ise* (ee-say), where the spirits of dead emperors are enshrined. The shrine is in such a beautiful location that Japan author Donald Keene once noted that its beauty alone was enough to ensure faith in the Shinto gods. The buildings of the Ise Shrine are rebuilt every twenty years. They were rebuilt for the sixtieth time in 1973.

Along with its emphasis on fertility, Shintoism also incorporates a deep respect for the soul of man, a view of mankind as brothers responsible for each other's welfare and happiness, and a vision of complete tranquility and peace.

All of the well over 100,000 Shinto shrines in Japan are marked by the presence of a *torii* (toe-ree), the familiar "gate" consisting of two upright columns and one or two pieces across the top, depending on the style. Shinto priests wear robes of white or pastel colors (Buddhist priests wear black). Worshipers do not enter the shrine when paying their respects. They simply bow before the shrine and clap their hands to attract the attention of the enshrined spirit or god before making a silent prayer, then make an offering of money to the shrine coffers.

The Buddhist Theme

Buddhism was introduced into Japan from China in the sixth century A.D., and over the next several hundred years most Japanese became Buddhists as well as Shintoist. Buddhism had a profound influence on the culture and civilization of Japan, serving as the medium for the introduction of new ideas regarding handicrafts, architecture, art, wearing apparel, festivals, burial customs, and perhaps most important of all, a system of writing, which led to the beginning of written literature. Buddhism also introduced, particularly in the twelfth and thirteenth centuries, new ways of looking at the questions of life and death.

One of these new approaches to living was bound up in the Zen sect of Buddhism, which in simple terms aims at bringing the body, mind, and spirit into perfect harmony with each other and the world at large. Zen teaches that this goal is to be achieved by first gaining control of the mind, conditioning it to perceive things as they really are, then making one's life an extension of this knowledge.

Zen thereafter became the leavening in the distinctive character of the Japanese civilization, providing them with another philosophy, another ethical foundation, a final arbiter in matters of taste, and a means of gaining extraordinary mastery in such skills as calligraphy, painting, gardening, utensil-making, and even swordfighting.

Under the influence of Zen, the Japanese strove to perfect a "cult" of spiritual and intellectual tranquility and to recognize the true essence of things by means of continuous self-discipline and control over their emotions and desires. They made many of the ordinary actions of life into exercises in mental control and composure, and developed a series of special exercises aimed at making perfect tranquility a permanent state of mind.

The Confucian Theme

Confucianism, a semireligious ethic system also introduced into Japan from China (some authorities say in 285 A.D.), was responsible for the establishment in Japan of what has been referred to as "the cult of the family," which taught that filial piety was the highest virtue, and resulted in a form of ancestor worship.

This filial piety was owed to parents as well as to the sovereign, who was the symbolic father of all. The state was seen as an extended version of the family. Behavior toward superiors, equals, and inferiors was prescribed in a strict code of manners.

Confucianism taught that man was innately good (the opposite of Christianity?), and that he needed only instruction and example to behave properly and avoid evil—not threats and punishment, which are the hallmarks of the Christian religion. Confucianism was thus more compatible with the Japanese than Buddhism, and gradually pushed the latter into the background. Confucianism is credited with giving impetus to a renaissance of learning and refinement of the Japanese culture that took place during the 265-year reign of the Tokugawa feudal government (1603–1868).

While most Japanese today do not claim any particular religious affiliation, Japanese culture as a whole is a mixture of Shintoism, Buddhism, and Confucianism. All of Japan's hundreds of festivals and ceremonial functions that are so much a part of the life of every Japanese are derived from one or another of these three streams of thought. At the same time, there are several Buddhist-oriented sects that have active memberships numbering in the millions.

The Aesthetic Theme

For some unknown reason, the Japanese were very early endowed with an extraordinary regard for natural beauty. Other cultures have developed within scenic surroundings but none except the Japanese has ever made the appreciation of beauty into a national pastime and an art in itself. As noted in my *Japanese Secrets of Graceful Living*: "From earliest times the Japanese engaged in regular exercises for developing their aesthetic sense and for appreciating beauty—a phenomenon so unusual in the world that this alone would have been enough to make them unique."

It was apparently their highly developed regard for nature and their devotion to natural beauty that led the Japanese to fashion a culture in which a natural type of functional beauty became characteristic of their tools, utensils, handicrafts, decorative items, and buildings. Ordinary bowls and trays produced over two thousand years ago for everyday kitchen or household use had what we now refer to as classical beauty. This output of highly artistic utilitarian products is said to have been "prodigious" by the eighth century.

Whatever its source, this preoccupation with beauty, refined by Zen concepts to the essence of naturalness and simplicity, is one of the most powerful and conspicuous themes of life in Japan. The adoration of beauty as seen in nature reached its climax in the various blossom-viewing practices and especially in the tea ceremony, where the practice of aesthetics is combined with a physical and mental discipline based on a total philosophy of life.

The Tea Ceremony

In fact, Japan's extraordinary dedication to aesthetics became epitomized in the now famous—but often misunderstood—*Cha-no Yu* or "tea ceremony." In their cultural shortsightedness, many of the first Westerners to visit Japan discounted and criticized the tea ceremony because they didn't like the taste of the tea that was served.

The tea ceremony, already a popular "cult" in the sixteenth century, has as its primary purpose the teaching of gracefulness and inner harmony, the understanding and appreciation of true beauty, and finally, recognition and appreciation of man's relation with nature.

A typical tea ceremony includes a tea master or student of the art and a few guests. The host makes all of the preparations in advance, in a small room or detached house designed and built for the purpose. Customarily the guests enter the room in the order of their reputation for cultural refinement, their age, or their relationship with the host.

There is no talking. The aim is to achieve complete physical and mental relaxation. When the tea is ready, the host serves the guests in a ceremonial manner dating back to the time of the great tea master Sen-no Rikyu (1521–1591). Then the ranking guest asks permission to examine the tea implements. These are placed in front of the guests, who attempt to merge their consciousness with the simple naturalness and beauty of the implements.

The host then bows his guests out, prepares a cup of tea for himself, and, as described in *Japanese Secrets of Graceful*

Living, "drinks it in solitude, savoring the thick, astringent brew, the quiet lonely mood, and the setting until the last measure of aesthetic joy is his."

There are a number of *Cha-no Yu* "schools" in Japan today, all doing a flourishing business. Two of the best known are *Omote Senke* (oh-moe-tay sain-kay) and *Ura Senke* (uu-rah sain-kay), originally founded in Kyoto by the same tea master, and then split into separate schools by the master's descendants—at first in the same building (*omote* means "front" and *ura* means "back"), where they were lodged for a long time.

The Japanese Concept of Beauty

The distinctive Japanese concept of beauty came to be described by the term *shibui* (she-booey), which means something like "astringent" and "restrained," and refers to a stark simplicity and naturalness that reveals the essence of a thing.

To the Japanese, beauty and naturalness are practically synonymous. Anything that is unnatural cannot be beautiful, but at the same time, beauty may be enhanced by accenting certain natural qualities.

The Japanese are especially sensitive to signs of age, such as the bleached color of driftwood, moss on a rock or tree, the twisted body of an ancient pine tree, or the parched, wrinkled face of an old person.

The Japanese express the appearance and feeling of age by the word *sabi* (sah-bee) which literally means "rust." To them, objects that are "rusty" with age are particularly beautiful. Japanese craftsmen deliberately build this quality into many of their wares.

Another quality of beauty as seen by the Japanese is expressed by the term *wabi* (wah-bee), which is an abbreviation of *wabishi* (wah-bee-she) and means "wretched, desolate," or "lonely." A further quality that the Japanese demand in beauty is one that lies below the surface in a very delicate harmony that is visible only to the person whose aesthetic abilities are highly trained. This quality is often referred to as *yugen* (yuu-gain), which means "mystery" or "subtlety."

Finally, there is another ancient Japanese word that is intimately linked with their view of beauty. This is *myo* (me-yoe), which might be described as the "soul" of an object, and which usually cannot be perceived by anyone with a strong ego.

With the Japanese, the practice of aesthetics was never a sometime or part-time thing. For centuries it permeated every aspect of their lives—from the arrangement of food on a serving tray or table to the decorations on their sliding wall panels.

The *tokonoma* (toe-koe-no-mah) is another thing unique to Japan. It began as an alcove-shrine in the main room of homes. By the fifteenth century it had become a special area reserved for the display of different art objects—one at a time and changed with the occasion or season. Japan thus became the only country in the world in which every home, no matter how modest or mean, had a place permanently set aside for the display of beauty.

The appreciation of beauty and the rules by which true beauty is judged are no longer overriding themes in the lives of the average Japanese, but they are still very much in evidence. Aestheticism continues unabated in the side of Japanese life that is traditional, and its influence makes itself felt in many areas of Japanese life that are Western. Tokyo's finest hotels, for example, owe much of their distinctive attraction to a subtle blending of Western-style accommodations and traditional Japanese concepts of interior decoration.

On a very practical level, the aesthetic traditions and conditioning of the Japanese make them very sensitive to the appearance and quality of all the modern-day products they make and buy—which is one of the reasons products made in the West with less attention to design and quality do not sell better in Japan.

"Living Flowers"

Probably the best known of the techniques the Japanese developed to train and practice their aesthetic abilities is the so-called "flower arranging," or *Ike Bana*, which literally means "Living Flowers." Ike Bana is said to date from a suggestion made by Emperor Saga in the ninth century, and still today no Japanese girl is considered educated until she has gained some skill in this gentle art.

The techniqe of *Ike Bana* consists of arranging flowers in such a way that they seem to be alive and growing. In doing so, the person is required to practice patience, gracefulness, correct manners, self-control, and peace of mind. Once arranged, the *Ike Bana* are displayed for a few days in the tokonoma, where all can appreciate them and reflect on their silent message of beauty and serenity.

The Artistic Impulse

The people of traditional Japan did not try to live apart from nature or to change it. Their aim was to live with it in harmony. The architect, on whatever level, designed his buildings to merge in with the surroundings. The craftsman accented the natural characteristics of his materials. The artist tried to capture the essence of nature by emphasizing its principal outlines and letting the viewer fill in the details from his own store of experience and imagery. The poet attempted to distill the essence of a fragment of existence by presenting a single provocative image of a natural phenomenon.

Until recent decades the Japanese were religiously trained in a number of artistic skills from childhood—not in a conscious effort to develop the skills for the sake of refinement, but because it was the natural way of life. One of the most important of these skills was learning how to write their own language—first correctly, and then with artistic style.

Before the appearance of a system of writing in Japan, there was an extensive oral literature. The people at large were great storytellers and versifiers. Then a remarkable event took place. The Japanese literally adopted the pictorial writing system of the Chinese, even though their spoken languages were completely dissimilar. Learning the complicated Chinese characters required years of meticulous study and practice by each person, and resulted in making the literate person, of necessity, an artist of considerable skill.

Afterwards, the Japanese developed their own simplified system for writing their language *(hiragana)*, which was gradually combined with the much more elaborate Chinese ideograms. But for one long period in Japan's history, education, social accomplishments, even a person's morality, were judged by how well—how beautifully—he or she could write the imported Chinese characters.

As more and more common people learned how to read and write, their penchant for oral versifying was transferred to poetry writing, which developed into a national pastime. The young and old, the well-to-do and the poor, the learned and the barely literate, composed, almost compulsively it seems, to satisfy their own poetic passions as well as to share their emotions with others.

Being able to dash off a clever and evocative poem became equated with the highest cultural achievements, just as the ability with the writing brush had in earlier times. The stern *samurai* warriors were as proud, if not prouder, of their poetry-writing skills as they were of their astounding swordsmanship. Cut down on the battlefield, a warrior would often use his last few seconds of life to compose and toss a wise couplet at his enemies.

Poetry-writing schools flourished by the hundreds in Japan until the modern era began, and men like Basho, Buson, Issa, Shiki, and Tansetsu won lasting fame. Poetry-writing contests were held and attended with all the enthusiasm that accompanies one of our greatest sporting events. Finally, an annual nationwide "poetry tournament" was inaugurated, and the tournament—open to everyone—continues today. Participants number in the dozens of thousands and include members of the imperial family down to grade-school students in remote mountain communities.

Singing was traditionally a part of the everyday life of the Japanese. Still today, many Japanese children can carry a tune and sing before they can talk well (because their mothers, grandmothers, and other family members are always singing to them). Most of them know dozens of songs by heart by the time they reach their teens, and are old hands at singing alone and in groups at parties and other festive occasions.

Singing was also closely associated with work in Japan. There were special songs, handed down for generations, for virtually every type of traditional job, and often differing with the region of the country. Sometimes, as in the case of farmers, fishermen, and carpenters, who are regularly called upon to do very hard work, these songs were ritualistic in nature and served to provide them with a rhythmic beat to follow in their movements. In other cases, the songs—and often singsong cries—were used by trades-men to identify themselves and their wares, a custom that continues today.

Get a group of Japanese together for any casual or re-creational purpose and they almost invariably end up sing-ing.

From earliest times, dancing was also an integral part of Japanese life. Children received informal instruction in how to dance at a very early age. By the time they were three or four years old, they naturally joined in the dancing at the frequent festivals. These folk-dances required the attainment of considerable grace, and until recent decades no Japanese—unless they were physically handicapped—could reach adulthood without being able to perform well enough in public to avoid embarrassment.

In addition to casual folk-dancing, classical dancing has long been a vital part of Japanese culture, and still today helps to shape the character and manners for which the Japanese are noted. Classical dancing is an integral part of several forms of Japanese theater, and is also part of the training of many young girls. The profession of dance teacher is an honored one, and there are many schools (styles) of dancing in Japan today.

Although the custom of everyone learning how to dance, by natural osmosis as well as formal study, has changed, particularly in urban areas and among boys, the vast ma-jority of the Japanese can still put on a pretty good exhibi-tion of folk-dancing when the occasion arises.

The Kindness Cult

Despite some contradictions in their character, the Japa-nese are among the kindest and most helpful of all people, especially when compared to some of the industrially advanced Western nationalities. In fact, this kindness, particularly where visiting foreigners are concerned, often goes so far it becomes embarrassing because we are not used to it and do not know how to accept it graciously.

The kindness of the Japanese is a traditional thing that is deeply embedded in their culture. In the earliest historical writings of the country there are frequent mentions of the importance of kindness, and kindness is one of the Five Principles of Confucianism making up the ethical base of Japan's traditional social system (the others were filial piety, fidelity, obedience, and loyalty to superiors).

It sometimes happens that the helpful concern of the Japanese is misunderstood by a certain type of foreign visitor. Not being used to such behavior, they tend to be suspicious of it or derogatory toward it. Most visitors, however, respond spontaneously to this too rare type of behavior with great delight and a feeling of wonder. In my years of monitoring the reactions of travelers in Japan, the thing that most impresses them—actually overwhelms them in many cases—is this singular Japanese trait of unselfish kindness.

The typical Japanese behavior manifests itself in numerous ways in all areas of life. But it is especially characteristic of the various services that make up the travel and vacation industry. It is not an exaggeration to say that in Japan the customer is king.

The Philosophy of Hospitality

The secret of the special relationship that exists between customers and proprietors, clerks, and other staff in Japan is bound up in the word *O'kyaku* (oh-kyah-kuu), with the title *san* (sahn) attached, which means both "honored customer" and "honored guest."

In other words, in the service industries especially, the Japanese do not distinguish between guest and customer. They treat a customer with the same high respect and deference that people elsewhere usually reserve for a visiting rich uncle.

This traditional custom is one of the many things that makes traveling in Japan such a pleasurable and rewarding experience. The traveler benefits enormously not only because of this custom, but also because as an outsider who is also a guest, his status is even higher than that of a rich uncle.

The foreign visitor in Japan is regarded not just as a guest of an individual, a hotel, or a particular restaurant or shop. He or she is also quite literally viewed as a guest of Japan, which means a Very Important Person whose comfort and satisfaction is a national responsibility.

As is well known, the Japanese are a proud people and are very much concerned with "face"—which, of course, is another way of saying "reputation" or how other people regard them. This pride and concern for face is both individual and national. Each Japanese feels responsible for his or her own reputation as well as that of the country. He or she automatically goes to extraordinary lengths to protect both.

The Japanese therefore tend to feel personally obligated to help every foreign visitor enjoy the trip and get only the best impression of Japan. To a certain type of foreigner this attitude and behavior smacks of sycophancy, inferiority, and even malicious cunning, but this reaction is in error.

The kindness and hospitality of the average Japanese is spontaneous and springs from inherent goodwill and genuine concern for people. Even when this special kindness is part of the travel industry's professional service, and is calculated and emphasized, it serves exactly the same purpose and sets the Japanese apart, as one traveler after another discovers shortly after arriving in the country.

CHAPTER IV

Nihon No Tanoshimi No Koto

The Joys of Japan

The Pleasure Theme

Pleasure has traditionally been one of the primary facets of Japanese life. Shintoism embraced the concept that physical pleasures, along with the intellectual and spiritual, were an integral part of man's existence. The Japanese have taken full advantage of this recognition since ancient times.

The physical pleasures indulged in by the Japanese cover a wide range and include sex, participating in festival celebrations, visiting hot-spring spas, eating, traveling, drinking (a *lot* of drinking), playing numerous games, hiking, and more. Their traditional intellectual pleasures include the already mentioned poetry-writing, attending the theater, and such aesthetic practices as flower- and moon-viewing.

Sexual Mores

In addition to the almost hypnotic aesthetic attraction that Japan has for sensitive foreign visitors as a result of its natural and man-made beauty, there is another attraction provided by a broad, deep stream of sensuality that flows through the culture. This sensuality, which gives off a constant promise of sex, acts as a powerful stimulant, particularly to foreign men visiting the country, coloring their view of Japan and its people. Of course, this sexual stimulation is magnified by the imagination of the visitors from abroad, but the promise becomes a reality often enough that Japan more than deserves its reputation for worldly pleasures.

As noted in my *Bachelor's Japan*, the Japanese regard sex as one of the several normal human activities that is to be engaged in regularly and completely as long as it is kept in its place. Recognizing sex as an important natural function in the overall scheme of life, the Japanese have never regarded it as evil. On the contrary, it is considered unnatural and harmful for a man or woman to go without satisfying sexual relations.

At the same time, there were different sex standards for men and women. Wives were primarily for the continuation of the family, while sex for pleasure and recreation was often indulged in outside the home. A man's duties as a husband and father were traditionally separated from erotic pleasures. Marriages were arranged and love was not a consideration. For a long stage in the history of the country, a personal attachment between husbands and wives, particularly in the upper classes, was seen as a detriment to a successful marriage.

The keeping of mistresses has been a traditional feature of Japanese life, and elaborate courtesan quarters were a familiar aspect of every city until prostitution was made illegal on April 1, 1956 (with a one-year grace period). Casual sex has lost none of its popularity in present-day Japan, however, and although organized prostitution must operate behind a facade of discretion, it flourishes on both a professional and an amateur basis. Personal liaisons formed strictly for sexual pleasure, and involving people in all areas of life, are also a characteristic feature of the current scene—although the AIDS scare that finally struck Japan in 1987 put a damper on some of the institutionalized activity.

Beginning of Western-type Nightlife

There is no country in the world today where the art of entertainment and the volume and variety of nightlife surpasses that of Japan. Most people are familiar with the terms *kabuki* (kah-buu-kee) and *geisha* (gay-e-shah), but these two institutions do not begin to suggest the range of Japan's remarkable entertainment industry.

Known in colloquial Japanese as *mizu shobai* (me-zoo show-bye) or literally "water business," the entertainment trades traditionally include not only show business as such but all the enterprises engaged in selling prepared food and drink to the public. The interesting connotation is apparently that earthly pleasures may sparkle brightly for a short while, but they soon evaporate into nothing.

In ancient times, entertainment in Japan was generally divided into two categories—one associated with eating and drinking (and often sex), and the other with various forms of theater.

Prior to the early 1920s there was practically no Western-style nightlife in Japan. Then Japanese travelers returning from Europe introduced cafés directly styled after French coffee shops. Before long these cafés began serving alcoholic drinks, and soon developed into the predecessors of today's cabarets and nightclubs.

Americans introduced Western-style nightclub entertainment into Japan during the 1945–1952 military occupation, and with the passing of the licensed gay quarters in April 1957 the world of the *mizu shobai* rapidly took on its present form.

Until the late 1950s Japan's extensive entertainment trades catered almost exclusively to men. Before this, men simply did not take their wives or girlfriends out nightclubbing. Female companionship was traditionally provided by large numbers of young women employed in the "water business" as hostesses, barmaids, and waitresses.

The Geisha Today

Geisha are still a very important part of the entertainment, business, and political world in Japan today, but there have been a number of fundamental changes in the profession. Present-day geisha in the great cities operate more or less as independent businesswomen who belong to a tightly closed association. Some of them live in geisha residences. Others live in ordinary homes or apartments and commute like any other working woman.

Guests do not ordinarily go to "geisha houses" as such. They patronize a special kind of restaurant-inn called *ryotei* (rio-tay) that calls in geisha as their request. There are some restaurant-inns, however, that employ live-in geisha on a full-time basis. As in the past, the purpose of the geisha is to entertain male guests by singing, dancing, and engaging them in light, often risque, conversation.

Both Japanese politicians and older businessmen say that geisha and cabaret hostesses as well add a special "soft" or "sweet" quality to the hard facts and serious decisions they have to make, and that is why they like to have these professional women on hand when they are wheeling and dealing or have just finished a hard piece of business.

The Shimbashi geisha district is one of the best known of the more than two dozen listed districts in Tokyo, and at the last count included seventy geisha *ryotei*. Guests who call in geisha are charged by the hour, with the rate depending on the class and popularity of the individual geisha. It is said that top geisha from Shimbashi as well as the Akasaka and Yanagibashi districts earn between $150,000 and $300,000 a year. But only a small percentage of this is net income because their expenses are very high.

Geisha generally work in teams of three or four. A geisha dinner party usually lasts from three to four hours and a bill of several thousand dollars is not unusual. Geisha from less prestigious districts are not as expensive.

Licensed geisha are not prostitutes, although it is common for them to form sexual liaisons with exclusive patrons.

In addition to the registered and licensed geisha, there are large numbers of women—often referred to as "instant geisha"—who are utilized by second- and third-class *ryotei* as well as by some traditional-style restaurants that cater to foreign visitors. These women do not follow the strict etiquette code of the professional geisha.

Coffee Shop Culture

Coffee shops play an important role in Japan, both day and night. Because the Japanese do not generally meet or entertain friends or business associates at home, and because there are no private offices in most Japanese companies, coffee shops are used as a universal meeting place in Japan. Some are small nooks that seat only ten or twelve people, while others cover entire floors of large buildings. Many coffee shops have distinctive themes that include the type of music featured, the uniforms worn by the staff, and so on. Some employ only good-looking women; others have all-male staffs. There are thousands of coffee shops in Japan's major cities, so the visitor generally has little problem finding one. The best guide is an outside sign—it may be very small and inconspicuous—that says "Coffee," since there is no telling what the front is going to look like.

After the visitor in Japan has dined, he has a wide choice of theater entertainment. Japan has been one of the world's top film producers since the 1950s, and there are over eight thousand theaters in the country. Several Japanese directors have gained international repute, and a number of Japanese films such as *The Seven Samurai* and *Rashomon* (rah-show-moan) are considered by many to be masterpieces of cinema art.

Most of Japan's entertainment districts include a number of first- and second-run theaters (the Rokku Amusement Center in Tokyo's Asakusa Ward boasts thirty theaters), and there are dozens of others scattered in main terminal areas. Some first-run theaters showing only Japanese films include English subtitles for the convenience of foreign viewers who do not understand Japanese.

Besides the movie theaters, Tokyo and Osaka have regular kabuki, noh, and bunraku or puppet performances. Kabuki plays are mostly classical dramas in which male actors perform all the roles while dressed in elaborately styled, colorful costumes.

The puppet plays of Japan are kabuki in miniature. The best puppet theaters and handlers have traditionally been in Osaka, while Tokyo is recognized as the kabuki capital. The visitor to Japan who fails to take in a kabuki performance has missed one of the world's most extraordinary theatrical experiences. Noh dramas are usually too elegant and symbolic for the general public, and most showings are attended only by private noh clubs.

Japan's two most famous revue theaters are the twin *Takarazukas* (tah-kah-rah-zoo-kahs), one in Tokyo just across the side street from the Imperial Hotel (it was the Ernie Pyle Theater during the American military occupation of Japan), and the other in Takarazuka City about an hour outside of Osaka and Kobe. The Takarazuka theaters feature hundreds of tall, beautiful girls (no males) in a variety of musical revues and dramas that attracts hundreds of thousands of people (mostly young girls) annually.

The Soaplands (Massage Bathhouses)

One of the largest and most conspicuous of Japan's pleasure industries is its so-called "Soaplands," or massage bathhouses. Most of the hundreds of soapland massage bathhouses are located in or near well-known entertainment districts. In Tokyo's Asakusa area alone there are some 150 (there are several along the expressway between Tokyo and the New Tokyo International Airport in Narita that are visible from the limousine buses serving this route). Most of the soaplands cater only to men, but there are others that welcome both men and women and some accept women only. In all of them the general routine is similar. The patron is given a steam bath, a hot-water bath, and then a lengthy massage by a girl dressed in halter-bra and shorts—followed by some kind of sex service if the patron desires it.

All of the baths have beer and soft drinks available. Many have adjoining restaurants and offer patrons hotel-type room service facilities. Many of the baths launder the patron's underwear while he or she is being bathed and massaged.

For the uninitiated, a detailed description of the soap-land routine should be useful. Most of the soaplands will accept reservations by phone. In any event, you go in and walk up to a registration counter, just as you do in a hotel. If you have a reservation and have arrived just on time, your masseuse almost immediately appears (she will be wearing a short robe over her bra and shorts) and escorts you to her private bath-massage room. If you are early or have no appointment, you may be asked to wait in a lounge area where there will be magazines and usually a television set.

The first thing you are instructed to do when you enter the tiny vestibule of the bath-room is to remove your shoes. Then the girl helps you undress and hands you a towel to wrap around your waist. She escorts you to a steam box, guides you into it, and closes the hatch-door, leaving only your head exposed. While you are steaming, she will check the hot-water bath, offer you beer or some other kind of refreshment, and wipe the sweat from your brow. When you indicate that you have had enough she will let you out of the box and direct you to enter the hot-bath.

After letting you soak for a few minutes, the girl then directs you to get out of the tub and sit down on a small stool. She then proceeds to scrub you from top to bottom, front and back. She rinses you off with numerous buckets of fresh hot water, towels you dry, then directs you to lie down on the massage bunk—usually face-down to begin with. She then massages you from your toes to your neck and fingertips for some twenty to thirty minues.

If you are going to be offered a choice of any of the special services for which the soaplands are famous, you will know shortly after she has you turn face-up. Her ac-tions will become intimate enough that there will be no doubt when the next move is up to you. The girls can invariably communicate well enough in English to make their services and their rates known to foreign customers.